I0796395

Donald Trump

Controversial 47th US President

Bradley Steffens

San Diego, CA

Printed in the United States

For more information, contact:
ReferencePoint Press, Inc.
PO Box 27779
San Diego, CA 92198
www.ReferencePointPress.com

LIBRARY OF CONGRESS CATALOGING-IN-PUBLICATION DATA

Names: Steffens, Bradley, 1955- author
Title: Donald Trump : controversial 47th US president / by Bradley Steffens.
Other titles: Controversial 47th US president
Description: San Diego, CA : ReferencePoint Press, Inc, 2026. | Includes bibliographical references and index.
Identifiers: LCCN 2025006058 (print) | LCCN 2025006059 (ebook) | ISBN 9781678212124 library binding | ISBN 9781678212131 ebook
Subjects: LCSH: Trump, Donald, 1946---Juvenile literature | Presidents--United States--Biography--Juvenile literature | Businessmen--United States--Biography--Juvenile literature | United States--Politics and government--2017-2021--Juvenile literature | United States--Politics and government--2021---Juvenile literature | LCGFT: Biographies
Classification: LCC E913 .S74 2026 (print) | LCC E913 (ebook) | DDC 973.935092 $a B--dc23/eng/20250505
LC record available at https://lccn.loc.gov/2025006058
LC ebook record available at https://lccn.loc.gov/2025006059

CONTENTS

A Striking Turnaround

On January 20, 2025, Donald J. Trump stood in the Rotunda of the US Capitol Building, raised his right hand, and took the oath of office as the forty-seventh president of the United States. The oath completed, Trump shook hands with Supreme Court chief justice John Roberts, who had administered the oath, then shook hands with outgoing president Joe Biden, the man who had defeated him by 7 million votes just four years before. He shook the hands of a few other dignitaries and then turned—triumphantly—to the crowd.

This moment represented a striking turnaround from four years earlier, when on January 6, 2021, Trump publicly urged his supporters to march on the Capitol as Congress was certifying the results of the November presidential election. As he had been doing for weeks on end, Trump again falsely claimed that the election had been stolen—that he, not Biden, had won the election. Responding to Trump's calls to "fight like hell,"[1] more than one thousand of his supporters forced their way into the Capitol. They attacked and injured US Capitol Police officers, rampaged through the halls, and desecrated the seat of American democracy.

Now, four years later, the building had been beautifully restored, and the crowd that greeted Trump was on its feet, cheering. The ovation marked a political comeback unlike any the nation had ever seen. Trump stepped to the microphone. "The golden age of America begins right now," he said. "From this day forward, our country will flourish and be respected again all over the world. We will be the envy of every nation."[2] With Biden and Vice President Kamala Harris, whom Trump had defeated in the November 2024 election, seated just a few feet away, Trump described his plans as president. Foremost among these plans was his determination to undo nearly everything the Biden-Harris administration had achieved in its four-year term.

> "The golden age of America begins right now. From this day forward, our country will flourish and be respected again all over the world. We will be the envy of every nation."[2]
>
> —Donald J. Trump

Exercising His Power

A few hours later Trump sat behind the Resolute Desk in the Oval Office of the White House, prepared to sign forty-two executive orders and proclamations. The people who had voted for him fervently hoped he would fulfill the promises he had made throughout his campaign. The people who had voted against him feared the very same thing.

One by one, Trump signed the documents. The first one was titled Initial Rescissions of Harmful Executive Orders and Actions. It revoked dozens of executive actions taken by Biden, including seventeen he had issued in January 2025, days before leaving

On January 20, 2025, Donald J. Trump raises his right hand as he takes the oath of office as the forty-seventh president of the United States. Standing beside him is his wife, Melania.

office. "The revocations within this order will be the first of many steps the United States Federal Government will take to repair our institutions and our economy,"[3] stated Trump's executive order. Seventy-eight Biden-era executive orders were wiped away with the stroke of a pen. Among them were several promoting diversity, equity, and inclusion, better known as DEI. The rescinded orders included Advancing Racial Equity and Support for Underserved Communities Through the Federal Government, Preventing and Combating Discrimination on the Basis of Gender Identity or Sexual Orientation, and Revision of Civil Immigration Enforcement Policies and Priorities.

Trump then began issuing his own executive orders. "This is a big one," Trump said, signing an order titled Designating Cartels and Other Organizations as Foreign Terrorist Organizations and Specially Designated Global Terrorists. He commented, "People have wanted to do this for years." He then signed a proclamation declaring a national emergency at the US-Mexico border. "That's a big one," he said. "A lot of big ones, huh?"[4]

Igniting Controversy

In the space of an hour, Trump began the withdrawal of the United States from the Paris Agreement on climate change, closed all federal offices for DEI, and proclaimed that for governmental purposes there are only two genders: male and female. He also pardoned more than fifteen hundred people who had been convicted of various crimes committed during the January 6 riot at the Capitol, including some who had violently assaulted police. For Trump's supporters, it was a dream come true. For his critics, it was a national nightmare. "The mass pardon sends a message to the country and the world that violating the law in support of Mr. Trump and his movement will be rewarded," wrote the editorial board of the *New York Times*, condemning the president's pardon for the January 6 rioters. "He used a mass pardon at the beginning of his term to write a false chapter of American history, to try to erase a crime committed against the foundations of American democracy."[5]

> **"The mass pardon sends a message to the country and the world that violating the law in support of Mr. Trump and his movement will be rewarded."[5]**
>
> **—Editorial board of the *New York Times***

One thing that Trump's actions did not do was surprise anyone. For two years, as he campaigned for president, Trump had traveled the length and breadth of the country, telling voters exactly what he planned to do if elected. Plus, Trump had been president before. Everyone knew what he stood for. The Biden-Harris administration had been in power for four years. Everyone knew what it stood for. The country made a choice on November 4, 2024. Trump received 3 million more votes than he had four years earlier. More importantly, Harris received 6.4 million fewer votes than Biden had in 2020—a decline of 7.7 percent from the Democrats' 2020 total. The voters wanted change, and Donald Trump was bringing it.

From Childhood Rebel to Young Millionaire

Donald John Trump was born on June 14, 1946, in Queens, New York, the fourth of five children of Fred and Mary Trump. Donald's childhood was shaped by the no-nonsense attitude of his father, a successful real estate developer and property manager. "The most important influence on me, growing up, was my father, Fred Trump," Donald Trump wrote at age forty-one, chronicling his meteoric rise as a real estate mogul in his book *Trump: The Art of the Deal*. "I learned a lot from him. I learned about toughness in a very tough business, I learned about motivating people, and I learned about competence and efficiency: get in, get it done, get it done right, and get out."[6]

> **"The most important influence on me, growing up, was my father, Fred Trump."[6]**
>
> **—Donald Trump**

A Legacy of Success

Fred Trump was likewise influenced by his own father, Friedrich Trump, an immigrant from Germany who made a small fortune as a restaurant owner and real estate investor in the 1890s during the Klondike gold rush in Canada's Yukon Territory. Having learned from his father that hard work and an entrepreneurial spirit could yield large financial benefits, Fred Trump was eager follow in his father's footsteps. He noticed that while automobile sales were booming, city dwellers often had no place to store their vehicles overnight. In 1921, at age sixteen, Fred built a two-car garage for a neighbor. Excited by the payment he received, the teenager wanted to repeat his success. Using the money he had earned, he began building garage components—walls, roofs, and doors—that could easily be assembled on any lot. He sold and assembled his prefabricated garages for fifty dollars each.

Building a Dynasty

After graduating high school, the young entrepreneur was ready to try his hand at homebuilding. Because of the paperwork and permits associated with real estate development, Fred could not be in business by himself until he was twenty-one, so he teamed up with his mother to form E. Trump & Son, a building company. In an interview with the *Bridgeport Post* in 1964, Fred said that he had borrowed $800 from his mother and built his first single-family home at age eighteen in the Woodhaven section of New York City's borough of Queens. He then sold the house for $7,600 and used the profits to build more homes. In addition to the modest family homes, Fred began to build larger homes in the tonier area of Queens that became known as Jamaica Estates. By the 1940s Fred had built more than twenty-five hundred homes in the New York boroughs of Queens and Brooklyn. A 1938 newspaper article in the *Brooklyn Daily Eagle* referred to Fred Trump as the "Henry Ford of the home-building industry,"[7] likening him to the early twentieth-century carmaker who had pioneered the mass production of automobiles.

In 1936, at age thirty-one, Fred Trump married Mary Anne MacLeod, a twenty-four-year-old immigrant from the Outer Hebrides islands off the coast of Scotland. The daughter of a fisherman, Mary had immigrated to the United States in 1930 at age eighteen to escape the crushing poverty that gripped her native land at the beginning of the global depression. She moved to New York City, where several of her siblings had also settled, and worked as a domestic servant until her marriage.

Fred and Mary Trump welcomed their first child, Maryanne, into the world in 1937. The next year, Mary gave birth to their second child, Fred C. Trump Jr. The senior Fred Trump began building a Tudor-style home for his growing family on Wareham Place in Jamaica Estates. Completed in 1940, the five-bedroom

Donald Trump was born in 1946, the fourth of five children of Fred and Mary Trump (seen here in a 1990 photograph). Donald Trump says his childhood was shaped by the no-nonsense attitude of his father.

house would become the childhood home of Maryanne and Fred Jr. and the couple's next three children: Elizabeth, born in 1942; Donald, born in 1946; and Robert, born in 1948.

The future president spent the first four years of his life in the Wareham Place home. Meanwhile, his father began building an even larger house on property adjoining the backyard. The family moved into the twenty-three room mansion in 1950.

The Realist and the Dreamer

Although the Trump family was wealthy, Fred was determined to teach his children the value of hard work. He put the boys to work pulling weeds at home and pouring concrete on construction sites. The children learned that nothing went to waste on Fred Trump's job sites. "My father would go and he'd pick up the saw-dust and he'd pick up the nails, the extra nails, and he'd pick up the scraps and he'd use whatever he could use and recycle it in some form or sell it,"[8] Donald Trump later recalled. Accompanying their father whenever they could, Donald and his younger brother adopted their father's thrifty ways. "Robert and I would tag along and spend our time hunting for empty soda bottles, which we'd take to the store for deposit money."[9]

Young Donald learned from his father to appreciate the monetary value of even the humblest items, but he did not share his father's obsession with all things practical and material. Even at a young age, he felt there was more to life than earning a living. It was his mother, Trump later wrote, who inspired him to dream big. "She was a very traditional housewife, but she had a sense of the world beyond her,"[10] Trump wrote. She had an appreciation for history, tradition, and the importance of social ceremony. Like millions of people around the world, she watched the television broadcast of Queen Elizabeth II's coronation for hours on June 2, 1953. Fred derided it as a waste of time. "Enough is enough, turn it off," Fred told his wife. "They're all a bunch of con artists."[11] Mary ignored her husband. "My mother didn't even look up," Trump recalled. "They were total opposites in that sense. My mother loves splendor and

Hidden Roots

In his 1987 book *Trump: The Art of the Deal*, Donald Trump stated that his paternal grandfather, Friedrich Trump, immigrated to the United States from Sweden. In doing so, Trump was repeating a long-standing myth created by his father, Fred Trump. In fact, both of Fred Trump's parents came to America from Germany. Although Germans made up the largest single ethnic group in the United States when Fred Trump was born, war propaganda during World War I and World War II stirred up anti-German sentiment toward German Americans. Fred Trump wanted to avoid any controversy that might hurt his business. As a result, whenever the topic of his family's roots came up, he said his family came from Sweden.

Donald Trump set the record straight in his 2000 book, *The America We Deserve*, stating that his grandfather came to the United States from Germany. When a reporter for the *Boston Globe* asked Trump about the discrepancy between his two books, Trump said that his father claimed to be Swedish because "our country was at war with Germany," and "being from Germany didn't necessarily play so well for a period of time."

Quoted in Madison Czopek, "Germany, Scotland, Sweden: What Has Donald Trump Said About Where His Parents Were From?," PolitiFact, August 7, 2024. www.politifact.com.

magnificence, while my father, who is very down-to-earth, gets excited only by competence and efficiency."[12]

Taming the Rebel

Fred and Mary enrolled all of their children, including Donald, in Kew-Forest School, the oldest private school in Queens. With fewer than three hundred students spread across the thirteen grade levels, the school offered small class sizes and individual attention. The students wore uniforms—the girls in white blouses and plaid skirts and the boys in white shirts and ties.

> **"We were cutups. He knocked lunchboxes out of people's hands, he liked to tug on girls' hair, he was a little [bit] of a jokester."[13]**
>
> —Paul Onish, childhood friend of Donald Trump's

Like many bright and precocious children, Donald had a rebellious streak. He questioned authority and enjoyed breaking the rules. "We were cutups," remembers Paul Onish, who was one of Trump's closest friends in school. Donald could also be a bully. "He knocked lunchboxes out of people's hands, he liked to tug on girls' hair, he was a little [bit] of a jokester."[13] According to Onish, he and Donald were two of the worst-behaved kids in their grade.

Recognizing the need for greater discipline in Donald's life, Fred and Mary decided to enroll their thirteen-year-old son at the New York Military Academy (NYMA), a boarding school in Cornwall-on-Hudson, New York. Founded in 1889, the military academy provided the structure and discipline that Donald needed. Initially resistant to the strict rules, Donald soon adapted. He became an accomplished athlete, participating in all sports but excelling in baseball.

> **"I stayed [at New York Military Academy] through my senior year, and along the way I learned a lot about discipline, and about channeling my aggression into achievement."[14]**
>
> —Donald Trump

Leadership opportunities at NYMA also allowed Donald to channel his natural assertiveness. He rose to the rank of captain, responsible for overseeing cadets and ensuring adherence to the academy's rigorous standards. In later

As a teenager, Trump attended the New York Military Academy. A 1964 yearbook photograph shows Trump in his military school uniform.

years, Trump often credited NYMA with helping him develop his leadership skills. "I stayed through my senior year," he later wrote, "and along the way I learned a lot about discipline, and about channeling my aggression into achievement."[14]

Learning the Family Business

Trump graduated from NYMA in 1964. NYMA is one of the leading prep schools in the number of graduates attending the service academies, but Trump was not interested in a military career. His interest was business. While his older sister and brother attended college out of state, Donald decided to live at home and commute to Fordham University, a Jesuit institution in the Bronx.

Dealing with Strength

In *Trump: The Art of the Deal*, Trump recounts how he learned to cope with a particularly strong teacher at the New York Military Academy:

> Theodore Dobias was a former drill sergeant in the marines. . . . If you stepped out of line, Dobias smacked you and smacked you hard. Very quickly I realized that I wasn't going to make it with this guy by trying to take him on physically. A few less fortunate kids chose that route, and they ended up getting stomped. Most of my classmates took the opposite approach. . . . They never challenged Dobias about anything.
>
> I took a third route, which was to use my head to get around the guy. . . . What I did, basically, was to convey that I respected his authority, but that he didn't intimidate me. It was a delicate balance. Like so many strong guys, Dobias had a tendency to go for the jugular if he smelled weakness. On the other hand, if he sensed strength but you didn't try to undermine him, he treated you like a man. From the time I figured that out—and it was more of an instinct than a conscious thought—we got along great.

Donald Trump and Tony Schwartz, *Trump: The Art of the Deal*. New York: Ballantine, 1987, p. 73.

After two years of a general education at Fordham, Trump applied to the Wharton School of Finance and Commerce at the University of Pennsylvania, widely regarded as one of the nation's premier business schools. "At the time, if you were going to make a career in business, Wharton was the place to go," Trump later wrote. "Harvard Business School may produce a lot of CEOs—guys who manage companies—but the real entrepreneurs all seemed to go to Wharton."[15]

At Wharton, Trump pursued a bachelor of science degree in economics. His coursework included subjects like real estate, finance, and management, which provided him with foundational knowledge for his future career. It also gave him insight into his father's success as a housing builder and manager. He frequently visited New York during breaks, observing his father's business operations and attending meetings to learn the intricacies of property development.

Trump's First Big Deal

While in college, Trump teamed up with his father to undertake his first real estate development project. He had learned that the key to making a profit on any transaction was to buy at the lowest possible price and to sell at the highest price the market would bear. In real estate, buying at the lowest price often involved purchasing properties that were in foreclosure. This refers to properties where borrowers have defaulted on their mortgage or failed to meet other terms of the loan and the lender has legally taken possession of the property. The lender can then sell the property to recover some or all of the debt owed by the borrower. Trump says that when he was in college, he would read the listings of foreclosures while his friends were reading the comics and the sports pages of newspapers.

In 1964, a particular listing caught his eye. The owners of a twelve-hundred-unit apartment complex called Swifton Village in Cincinnati, Ohio, had defaulted on their loan, and the Federal Housing Authority (FHA), which had insured the loan, had taken

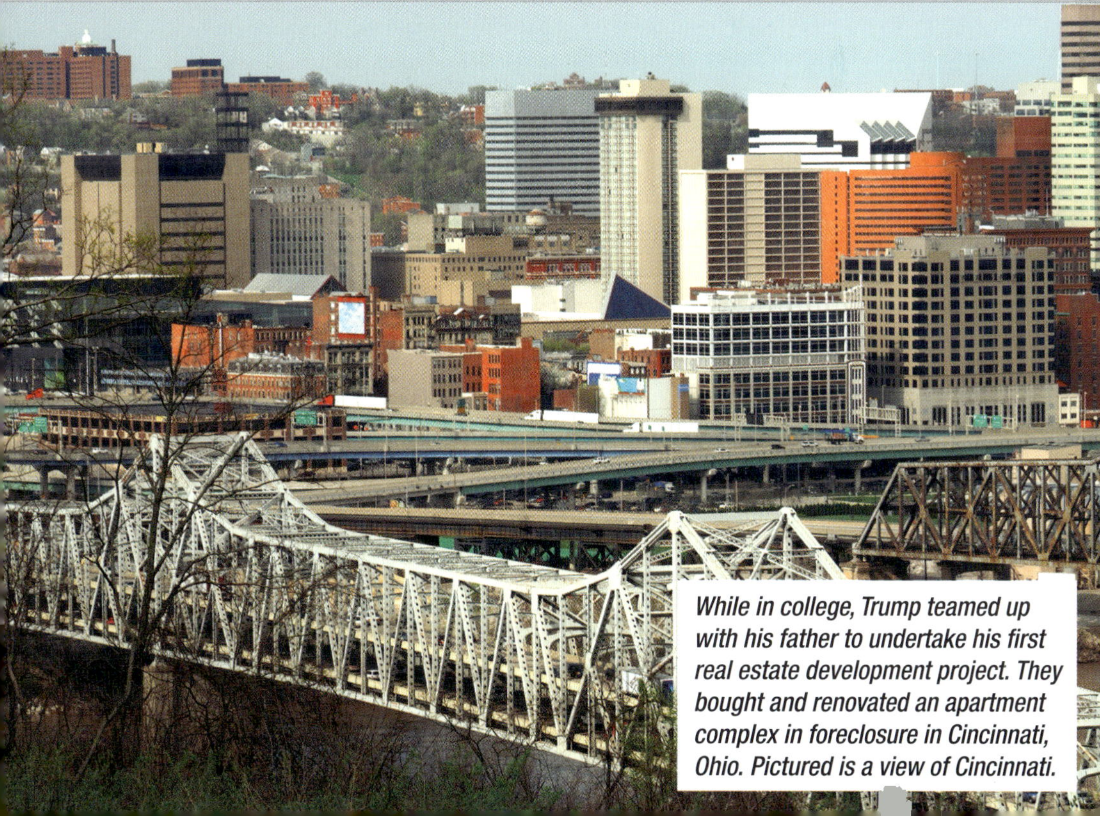

While in college, Trump teamed up with his father to undertake his first real estate development project. They bought and renovated an apartment complex in foreclosure in Cincinnati, Ohio. Pictured is a view of Cincinnati.

possession of the property. Trump convinced his father to put in a low bid on the property—just $5.6 million, less than half the amount the developers had paid to build it. With no other takers, the FHA sold the property to the Trumps.

Father and son secured a loan to buy the property plus have cash to fix it up. They employed local workers to clean, repair, and repaint the interior. They built a new community center, resurfaced streets and sidewalks, and installed new refrigerators and new laundry machines. They gave the outside a facelift, putting bright white shutters by the windows and installing attractive white doors to give the drab brick buildings a clean, homey appearance. The complex was two-thirds empty when the Trumps bought it. Even with a rent increase, it quickly filled with new renters.

The Trumps earned back their investment and made millions of dollars in rent over the next seven years. In 1972 they sold Swifton Village for $6.75 million, earning a profit of more than $1 million. Just as his grandfather Friedrich had made a fortune by building, managing, and selling restaurants in the Yukon Territory and his father had enlarged the family fortune by building homes and apartment buildings in Brooklyn and Queens, Donald J. Trump had made his first million dollars with a successful real estate development. And he was still in his twenties.

Trump's Early Career

Donald Trump graduated from the Wharton School in 1968. Unlike many of his fellow Wharton graduates, Trump was not interested in pursuing a graduate degree. Learning for its own sake did not appeal to him. More of a doer than a thinker, he felt that education was only important if it led directly to a career. His anti-intellectualism would later earn him the disdain of academics, members of the media, and even traditional Republican Party conservatives. However, it would also bring him the admiration and trust of millions of working-class voters who shared his low regard for academia.

Founding the Trump Corporation

With his undergraduate education complete, Trump decided it was time to enter the rough-and-tumble world of real estate development and property management. He began working in his father's business, Trump Management, full time. At the time, the company was primarily focused on developing and managing housing for middle-income residents in the outer boroughs of New York City. Donald started by working on smaller projects. Fred served as Donald's mentor, teaching his son the importance of cost control, efficiency, and negotiation.

The younger Trump immersed himself in the business, learning real-world lessons about project financing and construction, rent collection, and evictions. While Trump often squeezed subcontractors to get the lowest possible bids, he also came to admire their work ethic. He saw the pressures the small business owners and construction workers were under and the difficulties they faced. Construction is one of the most dangerous of all occupations, and Trump respected the courage and commitment of his workforce. Although born into wealth and privilege, Trump felt a kinship with the people who made his business grow. Later, he would champion the cause of working people as a growing number of American companies shuttered their US factories and moved production offshore.

In 1971, at age sixty-six, Fred decided to step aside and let Donald lead Trump Management. Two years later, in 1973, Donald renamed the company the Trump Organization, a tribute to his father and his paternal grandparents. He also viewed the company as a place for future generations of the Trump family to launch

After taking over the family business, Trump (pictured in 1982) renamed it the Trump Organization. He expanded the company's focus to include building and renovating skyscrapers, hotels, casinos, and golf courses.

their careers. Mostly, however, the name reflected the new image that Donald wanted to project for the company—one more in line with his mother's love of splendor and magnificence than with his father's competence and efficiency. "Somehow the word 'organization' made it sound bigger," Trump later said. "Few people knew that the Trump Organization operated out of a couple of tiny offices on Avenue Z in Brooklyn."[16]

> "Somehow the word 'organization' made it sound bigger. Few people knew that the Trump Organization operated out of a couple of tiny offices on Avenue Z in Brooklyn."[16]
>
> —Donald Trump

The Move to Manhattan

The Trump Organization's offices may have been located in Brooklyn, but its leader had his sights set across the East River, on the skyline of Manhattan. He rented a studio apartment in Manhattan and began to scout the area for properties to develop. His started by buying two abandoned railyard parcels from Penn Central Railroad. He planned to fill them with the kind of low-cost apartments the Trump Organization had built in Brooklyn and Queens. When the city placed a moratorium on new housing, Trump began to promote the Penn Central parcels as the ideal site for a new convention center, which New York badly needed. In the end, the city chose another developer to build the convention center, but it paid Trump a finder's fee for acquiring the land.

Trump's next move was to acquire and refurbish the rundown Commodore Hotel at Park Avenue and 42nd Street. He teamed up with the Hyatt Hotel company and commissioned an architect to create an innovative design. Trump had a hard time finding financing for the project until he convinced the city to hold off charging property taxes for forty years. In exchange, Trump would pay the city a yearly fee and a share of the project's profits. He would also pay back taxes on the property. The creative deal worked.

Instead of just refurbishing the inside of the hotel, Trump wrapped the building with reflective glass, giving the hotel a modern look. Some critics felt the design did not mesh with other

Fighting Back

Built in 1929, the Bonwit Teller building was considered by many to be an architectural gem. When Trump decided to demolish it to make way for his new skyscraper, he promised to preserve two 15-foot-high (4.6 m) limestone bas-relief panels that decorated the building's facade. His plan was to donate the panels to the Metropolitan Museum of Art. However, removing the stone panels proved time-consuming and expensive. When the demolition crew used masonry saws and jackhammers to dislodge the artwork, it crumbled. Trump was savaged by art lovers as a crass tycoon who cared only about money.

Stung by the criticism, Trump fought back. A spokesperson for the Trump Organization told a *New York Times* reporter that various art appraisers, who were never named, said that the limestone panels were of little value. Preserving them would have cost $32,000 and delayed the project by ten days. Asked about it years later, Trump inflated the numbers, saying removal would have cost $500,000 and delayed the project by months. Fighting back at criticism would become a Trump hallmark, alienating some who thought he behaved like a schoolyard bully but appealing to others who admired his fighting spirit.

buildings in the area, but the new Grand Hyatt Hotel was a success. It opened in 1980 and was soon earning $30 million a year in profits, of which Trump received half. More importantly, he had made his mark on the skyline he revered.

Building Trump Tower

Having proved himself capable of building on a large scale, Trump had no problem securing a $100 million construction loan for a project he had dreamed about: replacing the eleven-story Bonwit Teller department store at 57th Street and Fifth Avenue with a mixed-use skyscraper that would include stores, offices, and condominiums. "The main attraction was the location, but in addition, it was on an unusually large piece of property," Trump later explained. "In my mind, the combination made it perhaps the greatest single piece of real estate in New York City. There was the potential to build a great building in a prime location."[17]

While still building the Grand Hyatt Hotel, Trump teamed up with Equitable Real Estate, which owned the Bonwit Teller land, for fifty-fifty ownership of the site. Trump's contribution was to purchase the building for $25 million. He engaged the same architect who had designed the Grand Hyatt to come up with a forward-looking design for the fifty-eight-story building. The design included a zigzag glass-and-metal facade that added more visual appeal than a flat facade would have and gave the residents of the upper-story condominiums panoramic views in at least two directions. The extra views allowed Trump to charge even more for his luxury condominiums.

Trump Tower opened in 1983. It was an immediate success. According to author Marilyn Bender, 85 percent of the units were sold within the first six months, bringing in more than $260 million. This enabled Trump to pay off the $200 million in construction costs and make an immediate profit. Millions more rolled in from upscale retailers like jewelers Cartier, Harry Winston, and Buccellati that leased space on the first five floors of the glitzy skyscraper.

If the Grand Hyatt Hotel established Trump as a major developer, Trump Tower made him a celebrity. By the time the building was completed, millions of New Yorkers knew the name of the brash businessman. It was an image he cultivated through self-promotion.

The opening of Trump Tower in 1983 turned Trump into a New York celebrity and enabled him to cultivate an image as a brash businessman.

He courted the press, giving interviews and making himself available to comment on events. Not all of the publicity was good, but that did not bother Trump. In his view, negative publicity was still publicity.

Expanding the Trump Empire

As Trump's reputation grew, he began to frequent trendy New York night spots. He enjoyed mingling with politicians, business moguls, and celebrities. One of these clubs was Maxwell's Plum. There, Trump met Ivana Zelníčková, a twenty-seven-year-old fashion model from what is now the Czech Republic. Trump was impressed with Ivana's intelligence, charm, and traditional values—so much so that he proposed marriage. The couple's lavish 1977 wedding was the social event of the year in New York. "Ivana and Donald Trump were the 'It Couple' in New York City, seen as the very symbol of opulence, glamour, and luxury,"[18] remembers reporter Prachi Gupta. The birth of their children—Donald Jr. in 1977, Ivanka in 1981, and Eric in 1984—cemented their image as Manhattan royalty.

Soon the Trumps were being seen everywhere. The September 1983 issue of *Town & Country*, a lifestyle magazine appealing to upscale readers, carried a story about the young power couple. On April 8, 1984, the *New York Times Magazine* featured a lengthy story titled "The Expanding Empire of Donald Trump." Although mainly focused on Donald, the article spent eight paragraphs discussing Ivana's role as an executive vice president of the Trump Organization, focusing on interior design. A few months later, in September 1984, the television program *Lifestyles of the Rich and Famous* profiled Donald and Ivana's home, the three-story, fifty-three room penthouse in Trump Tower, bringing the glamorous couple into living rooms across the country.

By the mid-1980s Trump's properties included more residential towers, hotels and casinos, an airline, and even a professional football team—the New Jersey Generals in the United States Football League. In 1987 Trump gained further prominence when Random House published his autobiographical primer on negotiation,

Trump: The Art of the Deal, *published in 1987, reached number one on the* New York Times *best seller list and stayed there for thirteen weeks.*

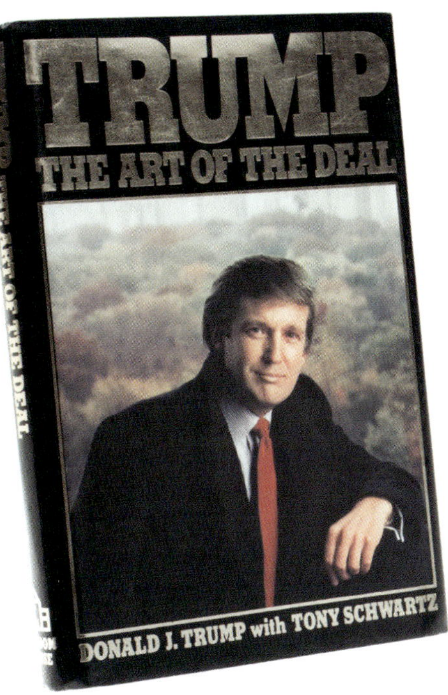

Trump: The Art of the Deal. Cowritten with author Tony Schwartz, *Trump: The Art of the Deal* reached number one on the *New York Times* bestseller list and stayed there for thirteen weeks. Profiled in numerous national magazines, including *Time* and *Playboy*, and featured on many television talk shows, Trump was becoming a familiar presence in American life.

Speaking Out for Workers

Capitalizing on his newfound fame, in September 1987 Trump took out full-page advertisements in three major US newspapers. These ads set forth his ideas about foreign affairs. He wrote that Japan and other countries were taking advantage of the United States. Under the headline "There's Nothing Wrong with America's Foreign Defense Policy That a little Backbone Can't Cure," Trump wrote: "The world is laughing at America's politicians as we protect ships we don't own, carrying oil we don't need, destined for allies who won't help."[19] These claims did not represent the complex nature of America's global partnerships, but they suited Trump's narrative of America as the victim of more clever and determined foreign leaders. He accused Japan of artificially suppressing the value of its currency. This, he claimed, was done to lower prices on Japanese goods. The ultimate outcome, he argued, would be lost American jobs when Americans bought lower-priced Japanese goods rather

> **"The world is laughing at America's politicians as we protect ships we don't own, carrying oil we don't need, destined for allies who won't help."[19]**
>
> —Donald Trump

Lessons Learned from *The Apprentice*

In 2004 Trump became the host and executive producer of *The Apprentice*, a reality television show. A ratings success, *The Apprentice* presented Trump as a tough, decisive leader, often ending each episode with the iconic line, "You're fired." A ratings winner, the program made Trump a household name. Former Speaker of the House of Representatives Newt Gingrich believes Trump's experience in *The Apprentice* did more than make him popular. It taught him how to communicate to a mass audience. In a 2024 interview on the PBS program *Frontline*, Gingrich said:

> Trump is very heavily shaped by television. He really likes television, and he thinks in television terms. . . .
>
> He spent thirteen years on television thinking about an audience. Only Reagan comes close to Trump in understanding media. And in some ways, Trump's experience was more direct. . . .
>
> He had learned early on, and I think *The Apprentice* really helped this, but he learned early on to talk in a language that was accessible by most Americans. . . . He talks at a level which is almost perfect if you want to maximize the number of people who will understand you.

Quoted in *Frontline, The Choice 2024: Newt Gingrich (Interview)*, YouTube, October 7, 2024. https://youtu.be/Uf_9vGpEC0M?si=v-UnUOzu7ZaYWJ8h.

than higher-priced American-made items. For a solution, Trump urged the federal government to place tariffs, a type of tax, on goods imported from Japan and other countries. "'Tax' these wealthy nations, not America," he wrote. "End our huge deficits, reduce our taxes, and let America's economy grow."[20]

During a discussion of these issues on *The Oprah Winfrey Show* in 1988, the popular daytime talk show host said, "This sounds like presidential, political talk to me."[21] Winfrey then asked Trump if he had presidential ambitions. He said he did not at that time, but left the door open to a possible future run "if things continued to go badly for the country."[22]

Three years later, author Patrick Buchanan, who had served as a consultant to president Ronald Reagan, echoed Trump's views on international trade and jobs. In his challenge to incumbent president George H.W. Bush for the Republican nomination in 1992, Buchanan said of Bush, "He is a globalist and we are nationalists. He would put America's wealth and power at the service of some vague New World Order; we will put America first."[23] Buchanan failed in his bid for the nomination, but his "America first" message was echoed by plainspoken billionaire Ross Perot, who made a third-party bid for the White House the same year.

Like Buchanan and Trump, Perot criticized politicians in both parties for not caring enough about American workers. Perot opposed the North American Free Trade Agreement (NAFTA) on the grounds that low-cost goods from Mexico and Canada (referred to in the business world as imports) would outsell American-made products. This would force American manufacturers to cut back production and lay off workers. Although Perot failed to win any electoral votes in the general election, he did receive 19.7 million votes, nearly 20 percent of the popular vote.

"We will put America first."[23]

—Patrick Buchanan, presidential candidate

Anyone who could count votes could see that millions of working-class Americans had lost confidence in the leaders of the two major parties to fight for their interests. One of those taking note of Perot's success was another billionaire: Donald J. Trump. For the next twenty years, he would continue to speak out against policies that he considered to be hurting the working class. Finally, in 2015, at age sixty-nine, Trump felt it was time to do something about the problems he had discussed for so long. He decided to run for president of the United States.

Trump's First Term

On June 16, 2015, the raucous sounds of Neil Young's "Rockin' in the Free World" filled the cavernous atrium of Trump Tower. As the music played, Donald Trump and his third wife, Melania, rode down an escalator to the ground floor, waving to the crowd. The couple then joined Ivanka Trump at a podium festooned with American flags. Stepping to the lectern, Donald Trump greeted the crowd. After describing his take on the problems facing the country, Trump announced that he was running for president of the United States. He promised to address the economic crisis he had been talking about ever since his 1987 full-page ads in the *New York Times* and other newspapers: "A lot of people up there can't get jobs. They can't get jobs, because there are no jobs, because China has our jobs and Mexico has our jobs. . . . Sadly, the American dream is dead. But if I get elected president I will bring it back bigger and better and stronger than ever before, and we will make America great again."[24]

Few political observers took Trump's announcement seriously. Many thought it was a stunt—a marketing ploy to promote his businesses and his popular television program *The Apprentice*. Nearly everyone predicted his bid would fail.

Connecting with the Talk Radio Audience

One commentator took Trump's announcement seriously, however. "This is gonna resonate with a lot of people, I guarantee you,"[25] said conservative radio host Rush Limbaugh, who was reporting on Trump's announcement even as he was speaking. Limbaugh hosted the most popular commercial talk radio program in the United States, with as many as 20 million weekly listeners. Having taken listener calls on a daily basis for twenty-seven years, Limbaugh knew his audience shared his frustration with politicians. Remembering the campaigns of Patrick Buchanan and Ross

> "Sadly, the American dream is dead. But if I get elected president I will bring it back bigger and better and stronger than ever before, and we will make America great again."[24]
>
> —Donald Trump

Perot, Limbaugh knew his listeners longed for a political outsider who was willing to fight for them.

Limbaugh was not the only talk radio host to see potential in Trump's candidacy. Sean Hannity, Michael Savage, and Laura Ingraham—each with millions of weekly listeners—also supported the brash New York businessman. While pundits in the mainstream media saw Trump as a neophyte who stood no chance, the conservative talk radio hosts saw someone who could step onto the political battlefield with an army of millions at his back.

It did not take long for the "America first" wing of the Republican Party to coalesce around Trump. Before his formal announcement, opinion polls showed Trump with the support of about 4 percent of Republican voters. After his announcement, Trump's support surged. A Suffolk University/*USA Today* survey taken one month after his announcement found Trump leading the nationwide Republican presidential poll with 17 percent support. This put him ahead of the established Republican politicians in the race, including former Florida governor Jeb Bush with 14 percent support, Wisconsin governor Scott Walker with 8 percent, and Texas senator Ted Cruz with 6 percent. Trump's skillful use of social media allowed him to continue growing a base of supporters. He ultimately won the Republican nomination, a feat many had doubted was possible at the beginning of the campaign.

An Electoral College Win

In the general election, Trump faced Democratic nominee Hillary Clinton, a former First Lady, US senator, and secretary of state with decades of political experience. Trump portrayed Clinton as a career politician who had done nothing to help the working class. He also said Clinton was part of a corrupt political establishment, which he called "the Swamp." His slogan "Drain the Swamp" capitalized on widespread antiestablishment sentiments held by not only Republicans but also many independent voters.

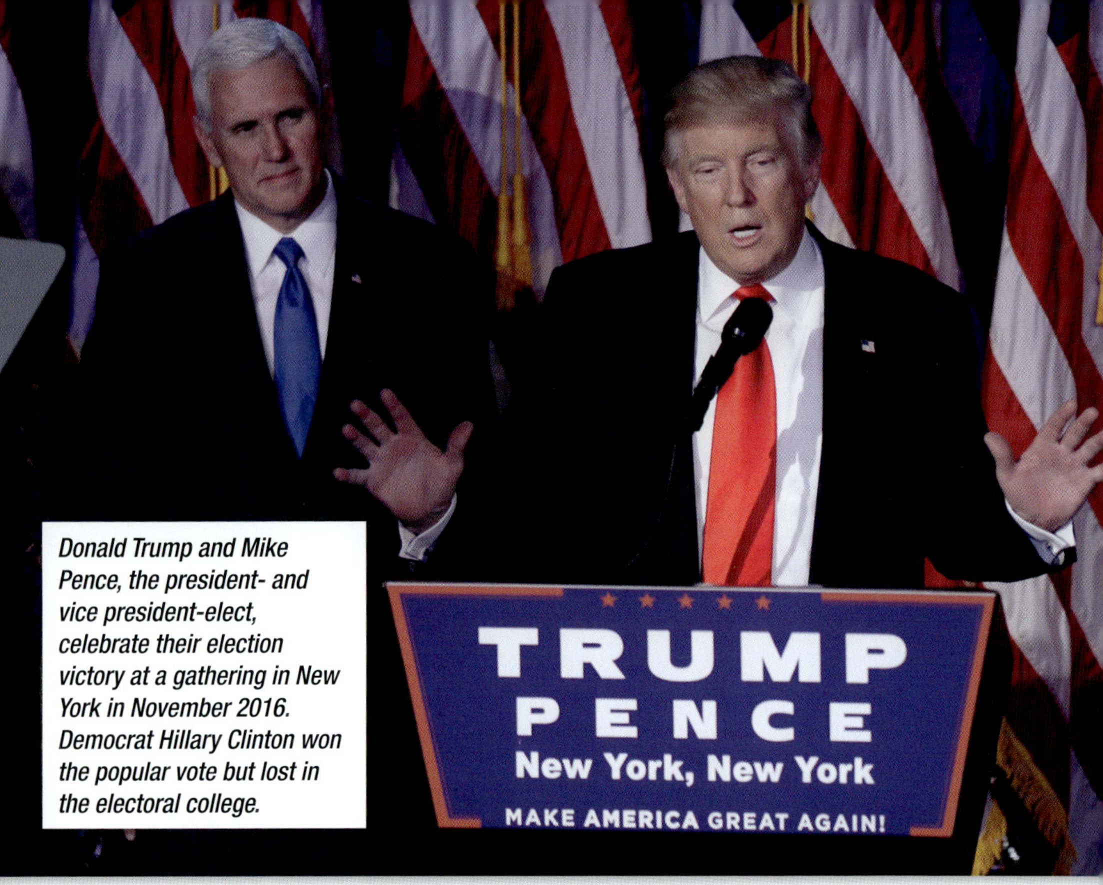

Donald Trump and Mike Pence, the president- and vice president-elect, celebrate their election victory at a gathering in New York in November 2016. Democrat Hillary Clinton won the popular vote but lost in the electoral college.

Trump's combative and often crude remarks limited his appeal in the general election. He won 46 percent of the vote. Clinton outperformed him, garnering 48 percent of the vote. She defeated Trump by nearly 3 million votes in the 2016 presidential popular vote. However, much of Trump's support was located in the battleground states in the Midwest, including Wisconsin, Michigan, and Pennsylvania. In these states his "America first" stance on trade and jobs appealed to blue-collar voters. Trump swept the battleground states on election day. Adding these traditionally Democratic states to Republican strongholds in the South and West, Trump secured 304 Electoral College votes, 34 more than the 270 votes needed to win the election.

Meeting Resistance

When Trump was inaugurated on January 20, 2017, he assumed he would have the full support of his party, since he had returned it to executive power for the first time in eight years. He was wrong. Many Republicans did not agree with the controversial billionaire's proposed policies. Despite having a majority in both the House of Representatives and the Senate, Republicans failed to pass some of Trump's major bills. For example, a bill to repeal the Affordable Care Act, a law passed under President Barack Obama that expanded access to health care for Americans, passed the House but failed in the Senate. Similarly, Trump had promised to build a wall on the US-Mexico border to reduce illegal immigration, but Congress refused to fund it.

The only major initiative Trump was able get through Congress was the Tax Cuts and Jobs Act (TCJA), which cut individual and corporate income taxes. In a speech in 2018, Trump said: "We have the biggest tax cut in history, bigger than the Reagan tax cut. Bigger than any tax cut."[26] Like many things Trump said, his boast was an exaggeration. TCJA was the largest tax cut for corporations in US history, but the combined cuts for corporations and individuals made it only the fourth-largest tax cut in US history.

> **"We have the biggest tax cut in history, bigger than the Reagan tax cut. Bigger than any tax cut."[26]**
>
> **—Donald Trump**

Executive Action

Without the backing of his own party in Congress, Trump began to issue executive orders to carry out his campaign promises. Having pledged to protect American jobs, Trump imposed tariffs (or taxes) on imports from China, the European Union, Canada, and Mexico. He replaced NAFTA, which he had criticized for years, with the US-friendly United States–Mexico–Canada Agreement. He also withdrew the United States from the Paris Agreement on climate change. This is the landmark international treaty aimed at limiting the dangerous rise of global temperatures. Trump insisted the agreement penalized the United States for its greenhouse gas emissions but did not penalize other major emitters, including China and India.

In the 2018 midterm elections, the Democrats gained forty seats in the House of Representatives, further blocking Trump's legislative agenda. Without the backing of Congress, Trump used his presidential powers to try to slow immigration at the southern border. He threatened to place massive tariffs on goods imported from Mexico unless the Mexican government agreed to prevent caravans of migrants from Central and South America from reaching the United States. In June 2019 the Mexican government agreed to step up immigration enforcement and to take in more migrants waiting for their US asylum hearings. This practice became known as the Remain in Mexico policy. As a result of these and other policies, apprehensions of undocumented immigrants dropped steadily through the second half of 2019 and into 2020.

By the end of 2019, Trump's policies were having positive effects on the economy. According to the Council of Economic Advisers, an agency within the federal government, the United States gained 7 million new jobs under Trump, causing the unemployment rate to fall to 3.5 percent, the lowest rate in fifty years. The shortage of unemployed workers drove up wages. Median household income increased by 9.7 percent, reaching an all-time high of $68,700. Importantly to Trump's base, wages rose fastest for low-income and blue-collar workers—a 16 percent wage increase.

The Challenge of COVID-19

With the economy up and illegal immigration down, Trump's reelection prospects for 2020 looked good. But unknown to Trump or anyone else, events in China would change the entire picture. On December 31, 2019, a municipal health commission in Wuhan, China, reported a cluster of unusual, suspected pneumonia cases to the World Health Organization (WHO). One week later Chinese authorities identified a new, or novel, coronavirus as the cause of these illnesses. On February 11, 2020, the WHO named the new disease caused by this virus COVID-19.

The WHO's January 30 situation report stated that there were 7,818 confirmed cases of COVID-19 worldwide. Most cases were in China, but 82 had been reported in eighteen countries outside China. One of those countries was the United States, where the

Trump Gets a Lucky Break

In the 2016 primaries, Trump's Republican opponents were confident that the star of *The Apprentice* would not be able to hold his own in a serious debate. In the first debate, Trump caught a lucky break when Fox News moderator Megyn Kelly asked him about disparaging comments he had made about women. Trump tried to make light of the subject, but when Kelly pressed him, the candidate made a remark that resonated with his supporters. "I think the big problem this country has is being politically correct," he said. "I don't frankly have time for total political correctness. And to be honest with you, this country doesn't have time either. This country is in big trouble. We don't win anymore. We lose to China. We lose to Mexico both in trade and at the border. We lose to everybody."

His answer made attacks on his character and language look trivial compared to what he described as much larger problems facing the nation. A Fox News poll taken after the debate found that Trump's supporters stuck with him. He continued to lead the field, even though a majority of those surveyed said he had the worst debate performance and believed he was the least likable Republican candidate.

Quoted in Rev, "First 2015 Republican Primary Debate Transcript: Classic Debates from 2016 Election Cycle," January 30, 2025. www.rev.com.

first COVID-19 case was identified on January 20, 2020. By March 12 there were 1,645 people from 47 states who had been infected with the virus that causes COVID-19. The next day, Trump declared the COVID-19 outbreak to be a national emergency. He empowered the US Department of Health and Human Services to temporarily waive or modify certain regulatory requirements so it could respond to the pandemic more quickly and effectively.

By October 2020, deep into Trump's reelection campaign, the pandemic had sickened more than 7 million Americans and killed nearly 207,000. Businesses had closed and millions were unemployed. All of Trump's economic gains had evaporated. Meanwhile, his handling of the pandemic had been unsteady. He had downplayed the seriousness of the outbreak at the beginning, incorrectly predicted that it would disappear with the warm weather of summer, and promoted unproven treatments. Joe Biden, the Democratic nominee for president, promised to guide the country with a steady hand and shape his COVID-19 policies in accordance with proven science.

Mail Balloting and a Biden Victory

To prevent further spread of COVID-19, many states encouraged voting by mail. Some states adopted full vote-by-mail elections. Others loosened their restrictions on mail-in ballots. For months before the election, Trump warned that switching to mail-in ballots without purging the voter rolls of ineligible voters would increase the potential for voter fraud. He provided no evidence to support this claim but continued to speak out against mail-in balloting.

More than 67 million mail-in ballots were cast in 2020, twice the number in 2016. The vast number of mail-in ballots proved impossible to count on Election Day, November 3, 2020. Several battleground states were unable to finish counting the mail-in ballots by that night. Having won Florida and other states with larger margins than he received in 2016, Trump was confident he would prevail in the battleground states. When Biden stated at 1:00 a.m. Eastern Standard Time (EST) on November 4 that he was "on track to win,"[27] Trump tweeted that Democrats were "trying to STEAL the Election."[28]

The COVID-19 pandemic had killed hundreds of thousands of Americans and sickened millions more by October 2020. Fear of further spreading infection led states across the country to encourage, or in some cases require, voting by mail.

Reshaping the Court

One of the most consequential accomplishments of Trump's first term was his appointment of three conservative Supreme Court justices: Neil Gorsuch, Brett Kavanaugh, and Amy Coney Barrett. Before Trump's appointments, the court had four liberal justices and four conservatives, with Justice Anthony Kennedy as a swing vote. When Kennedy retired in 2018 and liberal justice Ruth Bader Ginsburg died in 2020, Trump nominated Kavanaugh and Barrett to replace them. Their confirmation by the Senate gave the conservatives on the court a 6–3 majority.

Critics feared the conservative majority would jeopardize civil rights and the ability of women to obtain abortions. Some of those fears were realized in June 2022, when the conservative majority voted to overturn two precedent-setting decisions, *Roe v. Wade* and *Planned Parenthood v. Casey*, which held that the constitution guaranteed a woman's right to have an abortion. In *Dobbs v. Jackson*, the conservatives found that no such right existed in the Constitution and that it was up to the states to regulate abortion. Trump took credit for the court's action. "After 50 years of failure, with nobody coming even close, I was able to kill Roe v. Wade, much to the 'shock' of everyone," Trump posted on his social media platform, Truth Social.

Donald J. Trump (@realDonaldTrump), "After 50 years of failure, with nobody coming even close, I was able to kill Roe v. Wade, much to the 'shock' of everyone," Truth Social, May 17, 2023. https://truthsocial.com/@realDonaldTrump/posts/110384051064378318.

Leading the vote tallies in Georgia, North Carolina, Pennsylvania, and Michigan, Trump declared victory around 2:30 a.m. EST on November 4. Nevertheless, the counting of mail-in ballots continued for the next several days. The day after the election, the Associated Press (AP) declared Biden the winner of Arizona, Michigan, and Wisconsin. On November 8, the AP declared Biden the winner of Pennsylvania, giving him enough electoral votes to win the presidency.

Denying the Election Results

Convinced that tens of thousands of ballots had been cast illegally, Trump and his supporters challenged the results in various courts. Nearly sixty lawsuits claiming election fraud were dismissed, including two evaluated by the US Supreme Court. Unable to overturn the election results in the courts, Trump urged governors and legislators in various states to conduct recounts and decertify election results. He also called on Republican state officeholders to replace the elected Democratic slates of Electoral College members with Republican slates of electors chosen by the legislatures. When none of these maneuvers worked, Trump called on his supporters to come to Washington, DC, on January 6, 2021, to fight the certification of the election by Congress.

More than fifty thousand Trump supporters rallied near the Capitol to show their support for members of Congress who planned to object to the certification of the election results. Speaking on the Ellipse, Trump repeated his claims of voter fraud and added, "I know that everyone here will soon be marching over to the Capitol building to peacefully and patriotically make your voices heard." In the same speech, he stated, "We fight like hell, and if you don't fight like hell, you're not going to have a country anymore."[29] Following his remarks, about twenty-five hundred people illegally entered the Capitol Building to disrupt the proceedings. Many committed acts of vandalism and looting. They threatened members of Congress and violently attacked police officers who were trying to protect those members.

Rioters attack police and enter the US Capitol on January 6, 2021, in an effort to block certification of Joe Biden as the newly elected president. The rioters were responding to Trump's many false statements about the election being stolen.

Many people believed that Trump's behavior after the election and his speech on the Ellipse had caused his supporters to storm the Capitol Building. On January 13, 2021, one week before Trump left office, the House of Representatives adopted an article of impeachment against the president for incitement of an insurrection. Trump's trial began on February 9, 2021, and concluded on February 13. After hearing the evidence, fifty-seven senators, including seven Republicans, voted guilty. "President Trump incited the insurrection against Congress by using the power of his office to summon his supporters to Washington on January 6th and urging them to march on the Capitol during the counting of electoral votes," said Republican senator and former presidential nominee Mitt Romney, explaining his vote. "He did this despite the obvious and well known threats of violence that day."[30]

> **"President Trump incited the insurrection against Congress by using the power of his office to summon his supporters to Washington on January 6th and urging them to march on the Capitol during the counting of electoral votes."[30]**
>
> **—Mitt Romney, US senator**

Forty-three senators—all Republicans—voted not guilty. The vote fell ten votes short of the two-thirds majority needed to convict the former president. Trump was acquitted of the charges, but for many Americans, his actions after the election left a lasting stain on his presidency.

A Second Run for the White House

In the wake of the January 6 insurrection, Donald Trump did not seem like the person the Republican Party would want for a standard bearer in 2024. Once-loyal cabinet members like Education Secretary Betsy DeVos and Transportation Secretary Elaine Chao had resigned in protest over his actions on January 6. Some Senate Republicans who voted to spare him the humiliation of an impeachment conviction wanted nothing more to do with him. Even his own attorney general, William Barr, had turned against him. In a 2023 televised interview, Barr spoke about Trump's role in the January 6 insurrection. "There was very grave wrongdoing here. . . . Putting aside whether it is criminal or not, I do not see how the Republican party can nominate someone who is capable of doing something like that."[31]

"There was very grave wrongdoing here. . . . Putting aside whether it is criminal or not, I do not see how the Republican party can nominate someone who is capable of doing something like that."[31]

—William Barr, former attorney general for Donald Trump

An Unbreakable Bond

Once again, however, the leaders of the Republican Party had forgotten who had put Trump in the White House to begin with. It was not the party elites. It was his working-class base. These supporters did not feel betrayed by the defeated president. On the contrary, they were glad that he fought to the very end for what they believed was right. A CNN poll taken in the summer of 2021 showed that 72 percent of Republicans and Republican-leaning independents believed Trump's repeated claims that the 2020 presidential election had been stolen.

Realizing that Trump's base still supported the former president, California representative Kevin McCarthy, the Republican leader in the House of Representatives, visited Trump at his Palm Beach, Florida, home in 2021. McCarthy had said Trump bore responsibility for the January 6 attack and had recommended that Congress formally censure the president's conduct. Even so, he sought Trump's help in the next year's midterm elections. "McCarthy's visit really opened the door for Trump," says Meridith McGraw, author of *Trump in Exile*. "It was a permission slip to Republicans who had criticized Trump to forgive him and move on."[32]

"McCarthy's visit really opened the door for Trump. It was a permission slip to Republicans who had criticized Trump to forgive him and move on."[32]

—Meridith McGraw, author

Trump speaks at the 2021 Conservative Political Action Conference (CPAC), the largest annual gathering of conservative activists from across the United States. When Trump approached the microphone, the delegates erupted in cheers.

Buoyed by McCarthy's visit, Trump accepted an invitation to speak at the 2021 Conservative Political Action Conference, the largest annual gathering of conservative activists from across the United States. When Trump approached the microphone, the delegates erupted in cheers. "I stand before you today to declare that the incredible journey we began together is far from over,"[33] Trump said. He stopped short of declaring that he would run for president again, but the organization's traditional presidential straw poll suggested he should. More than two-thirds of respondents—68 percent—said they thought the former president should run again, with 55 percent saying they would vote for him in a Republican primary.

Ongoing Influence

The 2022 midterm primaries showed that Trump was still a force within his party. Republicans supported by Trump won primaries across the country, including Senate candidates J.D. Vance in Ohio and Herschel Walker in Georgia. His supporters used the primaries to take revenge on Republicans who had taken a stand

Surviving an Assassination Attempt

A pivotal moment in the 2024 presidential campaign occurred when a would-be assassin armed with an AR-15-style rifle fired eight rounds at Trump during a rally in Butler, Pennsylvania. Trump and three bystanders were struck by the bullets. One bystander, Corey Comperatore of Sarver, Pennsylvania, was killed. Two others were wounded. One bullet grazed Trump's ear just after he had turned his head to view a chart to his right.

Immediately rushed offstage by Secret Service agents, Trump raised his fist in a signal of defiance and shouted to the crowd: "Fight, fight, fight." Photojournalist Evan Vucci captured the moment in a vivid photograph. From Vucci's position, Trump's bloodied head and raised fist stand out against an azure sky with an American flag to the side. The photograph graced the cover of *Time* magazine that week. "Trump's reaction was genuinely extraordinary, because he didn't know if there were other shooters in that audience," observed journalist Piers Morgan after the election. "His natural gut reaction was to stand up and say 'fight, fight, fight,' with blood pouring over his face. I'm certain that, if there was any doubt, that's the moment he won the election."

Piers Morgan Uncensored, Tucker Carlson vs Piers Morgan, YouTube, January 30, 2025. https://youtu.be/qRO2NvIWCEY?si=8t5M7CoXtRTay0Kk.

against him over January 6. Four of the six House Republicans who voted for Trump's impeachment were defeated by Trump-backed challengers in the primaries.

Trump's support was not as decisive in the midterm general elections. Enough members of his party won their elections to return control of the House of Representatives to the Republicans, but it was by a smaller margin than expected. Several Trump-backed candidates won Senate races, but in Pennsylvania, Democrat John Fetterman defeated Trump's endorsed candidate, TV celebrity Dr. Mehmet Oz. As a result, a seat that had been held by a Republican became a gain for the Democrats, giving them a 51–49 edge in the Senate. Many Republicans who echoed Trump's belief that the 2020 election had been stolen were defeated in the general election.

Primary Challengers

The Republicans' weak performance in the 2022 midterms caused many to believe that the time had come for the party to move on from Trump. In particular, Florida governor Ron DeSantis—who had easily won reelection in his state—looked like a viable alternative to Trump. Biotech businessman Vivek Ramaswamy saw an opening for himself as another, younger political outsider to succeed Trump. Former South Carolina governor and US ambassador to the United Nations Nikki Haley thought the party was primed for its first female presidential candidate to broaden its support. Others vying for the 2024 Republican nomination included former vice president Mike Pence, Arkansas governor Asa Hutchinson, and North Dakota governor Doug Burgum.

Of the Republican hopefuls, only Trump, DeSantis, and Haley ever polled above 10 percent. A December 2022 *Wall Street Journal* survey showed DeSantis leading Trump 52 percent to 38 percent. However, by the time DeSantis formally declared his candidacy in May 2023, his support had fallen to 23 percent while Trump's had soared to 55 percent.

Entering the primaries, Trump faced numerous legal challenges related to his business practices and his attempts to overturn the 2020 election. He faced ninety-one indictments and was convicted of thirty-four felony charges. While Trump's opponents saw the convictions as proof that Trump was unfit for office, Trump cast them as politically motivated attacks. His supporters characterized the indictments as lawfare, a mix of the words *law* and *warfare*. This term represented the views of Trump and his supporters that the legal system had been used as a weapon to intimidate, harm, or delegitimize him. The legal challenges solidified Trump's support among voters who were skeptical of the establishment. Some Trump supporters proudly donned T-shirts emblazoned with his police mug shot. Others wore T-shirts that proclaimed: "I'm voting for the convicted felon."

In the Iowa caucuses, the first presidential contest of 2024, held in January, Trump received the support of 51 percent of caucus participants. DeSantis finished second with 21.2 percent, and Haley finished third with 19.1 percent. A week later, DeSantis ended his campaign. Haley continued to battle on but only defeated Trump twice—in the Washington, DC, primary on March 2 and the Vermont primary on March 4. Meanwhile Trump had won seventeen contests, including the primary in Haley's home state of South Carolina. On March 6 Haley ended her campaign, and Trump became the presumptive Republican nominee.

On the Attack

With the nomination virtually secured, Trump hammered Biden over a range of issues, especially the nation's inflation rate, which had peaked at 9.1 percent in June 2022—the highest rate in 40 years. During the COVID-19 pandemic, the production of many goods, including oil and gas, had slowed. When the pandemic passed, the US economy under Biden recovered quickly—more quickly than the economies of other countries. However, the production of goods and fuel could not keep up with the demand of people who had gone back to work. As a result, the cost of necessities such as gas, groceries, and utilities increased dramatically. When price increases over a given period lead to a lessening of spending power, this is known as inflation. The average inflation rate for the three and a half years of the Biden administration was 5.4 percent, while the four-year average under Trump was just 1.9 percent. Trump promised voters a return to the low inflation the country had enjoyed during his administration.

Trump also attacked Biden over his border policies. Those policies, Trump contended, were responsible for the massive rise in migrants crossing the US-Mexico border. From a low of 16,182 migrant encounters with US Border Patrol agents in April 2020 under Trump, the number had skyrocketed to 249,741 Border Patrol encounters in December 2023, the most ever recorded in a single month. Total nationwide encounters under the Biden administration exceeded more than 10.3 million, compared to just 3.1 million during the Trump administration. Trump tied the influx of migrants to the loss of jobs and stagnant wages of the blue-collar American worker.

Hundreds of migrants seek asylum at the US-Mexico border in May 2023. During the presidential campaign, Trump frequently attacked Biden's border policies. Trump blamed these policies for the rise in migrants crossing the border.

The Biden-Trump Debate

By March 2024 Trump held a 2-point lead over Biden—41.7 percent to 39.7 percent—in an average of polls conducted by data analysis firm FiveThirtyEight. The numbers hardly moved throughout the spring. Needing a boost to the campaign, the Biden camp challenged Trump to a series of debates, the first of which occurred on June 27. It was the earliest presidential debate in US history.

The two candidates sparred over inflation, deficits, immigration, and the war between Russia and Ukraine. Biden, who was eighty-one years old at the time, misspoke several times and had to correct himself. Then, answering a question about the national debt, Biden stumbled. "We'd be able to help make sure that—all those things we need to do, childcare, elder care, making sure that we continue to strengthen our healthcare system, making sure that we're able to make every single solitary person eligible for what I've been able to do with the COVID—excuse me, with dealing with everything we have to do with," Biden said. The president appeared to lose his train of thought. "Look, if— " he paused. Finally, he blurted out, "We finally beat Medicare."[34] Trump, who at age seventy-eight was just three years younger than Biden, pounced: "Well, he's right: He did beat Medicaid. He beat it to death. And he's destroying Medicare. . . . So he was right in the way he finished that sentence, and it's a shame."[35]

Support for Trump Grows

Misspeaking during a debate is not uncommon. Many candidates have done it. But Biden's lapse came across as something more serious than a simple gaffe. Trump and others on the right had been saying for months that Biden was showing signs of age-related cognitive decline. Biden, his press secretary, and other Democrats staunchly maintained that the president was as sharp as ever. They even suggested that questions about the president's mental state were a right-wing conspiracy. The debate revealed to the general public that the president's once-impressive speaking skills had diminished with time.

A Warning to Voters

In the closing days of the 2024 campaign, fourteen former Trump administration officials felt compelled to warn voters against putting the former president back in the White House. In an interview with the *New York Times*, John Kelly, the longest-serving chief of staff in Trump's first term, said that Trump met the definition of a fascist and would govern like a dictator if allowed. Two days later, thirteen other Trump aides sent a letter to the news website Politico, praising Kelly for sounding the alarm about Trump's fascist tendencies. "We applaud General Kelly for highlighting in stark details the danger of a second Trump term," the former aides wrote.

With polls showing a tight race, the Harris campaign met with a group of undecided voters to see what they thought of Kelly's remarks. The voters found Kelly to be credible and trustworthy, and they thought his warnings about Trump were important. Accordingly, Harris decided to emphasize Trump's unfitness for office. Throughout the last week of the campaign, Harris repeatedly referred to Kelly's letter in her speeches, especially the comments about Trump's admiration for dictators and his lack of respect for the Constitution and the rule of law.

Quoted in Meridith McGraw, "Ex-Trump Aides Emerge to Back Kelly's Harsh Warnings," *Politico*, October 25, 2024. www.politico.com.

Polls taken in the days before the debate showed Biden and Trump in a virtual tie. Polls taken after the debate showed Biden's support falling and Trump's rising. Prominent Democrats sounded the alarm that not only was Biden likely to lose to Trump, but his weakened candidacy might drag down other Democrats on the ballot. This, they worried, would make it impossible to recapture the House of Representatives and maintain control of the Senate. After initially saying he was not going to leave the race, Biden finally gave in to the pressure and stepped aside on July 21. He threw his support behind Vice President Kamala Harris.

A New Opponent

The Democratic Party officially nominated Harris on August 5, just two weeks after Biden had dropped out of the race. At age fifty-nine, Harris possessed an impressive political résumé. She had served as district attorney in San Francisco and then attorney general of California. She was elected to the US Senate in 2016,

Vice President Kamala Harris greets delegates at the Democratic National Convention in Chicago, Illinois, in August 2024. Harris became the party's nominee for president after Biden dropped out of the race.

becoming the second Black woman and first South Asian American US senator. As Biden's 2020 running mate, she became the first woman vice president and the first vice president who was both Black and of South Asian descent. In her speeches, Harris emphasized continuity of Democratic policies, arguing for social justice reforms, climate action, and expanded health care access. She framed Trump's return as a step backward for the nation. Her campaign often highlighted the need to protect democratic values, drawing attention to Trump's past controversies, including his ongoing refusal to concede the 2020 presidential election.

By early August Harris had risen from a virtual tie with Trump to holding a 2-point advantage in the FiveThirtyEight national polling average. This lead would hold throughout the summer and fall, although some polls showed Trump inching ahead in some of the battleground states. He continued to tie Harris to Biden so that he could portray the Biden-Harris administration as a failure on the economy.

Many experts believed that Harris needed to dramatically break with Biden to show she would govern differently than he did. Instead, Harris continued to tout the administration's successes. When asked by one interviewer whether she would have done anything differently than Biden, Harris said, "There is not a thing that comes to mind. And I've been part of most of the decisions that have had impact."[36]

Harris's answer fit right into Trump's message that Harris's and Biden's policies were the same. Within days, the Trump campaign was using Harris's words against her. In a thirty-second ad that ran in swing states titled "Four More," the Trump campaign showed a clip of Harris's answer on *The View* followed by a narrator saying, "Kamala wouldn't change a thing? Their weakness invited wars, welfare for illegals, while Americans struggle."[37] Once again, as he had ever since 1987, Trump portrayed Washington politicians as not caring about the working class.

"Kamala wouldn't change a thing? Their weakness invited wars, welfare for illegals, while Americans struggle."[37]

—Trump campaign television ad

Most public polls leading up to Election Day showed the presidential race was too close to call. Many feared the election would be a replay of 2020, with the result unknown for days and violence breaking out in the aftermath. As early voting began, the nation held its collective breath.

Winning the Presidency a Second Time

On September 20, 2024, early voting began in Minnesota, South Dakota, and Virginia. Later, other states followed. Historically, far more Democrats than Republicans vote early. In a major change in strategy, the Trump campaign urged Republicans to cast their votes before Election Day. Before Election Day, states could not report how many votes candidates had received, but some states could report how many members of each party had voted early. The numbers were astonishing. For the first time in history, more Republicans than Democrats had voted early in the battleground states of Arizona, Georgia, Nevada, and North Carolina. In Michigan, the parties were tied. Barring a last-minute surge by Harris, Trump appeared on the verge of winning back the White House.

A Big Night for Republicans

On Election Night, the leads Trump had built up in the early voting grew throughout the night. By 12:58 a.m. EST on November 6, the AP called Georgia for Trump. At 2:24 a.m. EST, the AP called Pennsylvania for Trump. With leads in Arizona, Michigan, Nevada, and Wisconsin, Trump declared victory. "I want to thank the American people for the extraordinary honor of being elected your 47th president and your 45th president," Trump told supporters at the West Palm Beach, Florida, Convention Center. "It is now clear that we've achieved the most incredible political thing."[38]

When all votes were counted, Trump had completed his political comeback. He held on to all of the states he had won in 2020 and won back the five battleground states he had lost to Biden in 2020: Arizona, Georgia, Michigan, Pennsylvania, and Wisconsin. He also won Nevada, a state that had not voted for a Republican presidential candidate since 2004. In all, Trump amassed 312 electoral votes, 8 more than he had won in 2016 and 42 more than needed to win the presidency. More surprisingly, Trump also won the popular vote—49.71 percent to 48.24 percent. It was only the second time in the previous nine presidential contests that a Republican had won the popular vote.

> **"I want to thank the American people for the extraordinary honor of being elected your 47th president and your 45th president. It is now clear that we've achieved the most incredible political thing."[38]**
>
> **—Donald Trump**

Trump also helped the Republicans hold the House of Representatives and win back the Senate. This governing trifecta—controlling the presidency, House, and Senate—was expected to enable Trump to achieve his legislative priorities. However, the Democrats held enough Senate seats to block legislation using the filibuster, a Senate rule that essentially requires a so-called supermajority of sixty votes to pass nonbudgetary legislation. Importantly, however, it would only take a one-vote majority to confirm Trump's cabinet picks, federal judges, and if needed, Supreme Court nominees.

Trump delivers a victory speech on election night in November 2024. He won both the popular vote and the electoral college this time around.

Naming a New Cabinet

With the help of his chief adviser, Susan Wiley, Trump was better prepared to govern after winning the 2024 election than he was in 2016. In his first term, Trump had been undermined by cabinet members who withheld information from him, refused to implement his policies, intentionally delayed or slow-walked his priorities, and leaked confidential information to Congress and the media. This time around, Trump was determined to fill key posts with people he knew and trusted. He also wanted to bring change to the various federal agencies and departments.

Instead of appointing experienced department officials, Trump filled his cabinet with outsiders, many of whom had been critical of the departments they would lead. For example, he chose attorney and activist Robert F. Kennedy Jr. to be the secretary of the US Department of Health and Human Services (HHS). For decades, Kennedy had spread false information about vaccine safety, in addition to criticizing the role and actions of the HHS. Trump selected Pam Bondi, the former attorney general of Florida and a vocal critic of the US Department of Justice (DOJ), to head that department as attorney general. Similarly, Trump tapped

Robert F. Kennedy, Jr., Trump's nominee to head Health and Human Services (HHS), testifies during a Senate committee hearing in January 2025. For decades, Kennedy has spread false information about vaccine safety and criticized the HHS.

Kash Patel, a longtime DOJ critic, to head the Federal Bureau of Investigation. And to head the US Department of Defense, Trump chose Pete Hegseth. Hegseth had served in the US Army for fifteen years. After leaving the military, he wrote two books and worked as a television host for Fox News. Critics questioned his lack of any relevant experience that would prepare him for running a sprawling government agency with an $841 billion budget and 3.4 million service members and civilians spread across 480 sites in more than 160 countries.

Trump's supporters applauded his choices. Trump had promised to replace Washington insiders with fresh faces who would shake up the existing departments and institutions. For some voters, this was the most important promise he had made. "I'm supportive of outsiders that don't have long Washington credentials," said Chris Hicks, a fifty-nine-year-old consultant in Cincinnati, Ohio. "The mandate to Trump from Trump voters, more than anything, is that we need to reform government."[39]

> **"Taken together, these appointments suggest an attempt to actually make the American government dysfunctional, to make it fall apart, to pervert it, to have it do things that it's not supposed to do until it's not capable of doing anything at all."[40]**
>
> —Timothy Snyder, Yale University history professor

Trump's critics derided his picks. "Each of them individually is historically bad," said Yale University history professor Timothy Snyder. "These are not people who are going to be bad at their jobs in some sort of normal sense. Taken together, these appointments suggest an attempt to actually make the American government dysfunctional, to make it fall apart, to pervert it, to have it do things that it's not supposed to do until it's not capable of doing anything at all."[40] Despite such criticism, the Republican-controlled Senate confirmed all of Trump's appointees.

Using the Levers of Power

In addition to installing new people to head departments within the government, Trump began instituting new policies through executive orders and proclamations. Some of the most consequential actions had to do with trade policy. Trump had long advocated the use of tariffs as leverage to achieve various goals, including gaining another country's cooperation, protecting American industries, and correcting trade imbalances.

On February 1, 2025, Trump placed 25 percent tariffs on goods imported from Mexico and Canada. The goal, he said, was to force the neighboring countries to cooperate with the United States on border security. The leaders of both Mexico and Canada immediately contacted Trump to say they would cooperate to better secure their borders. Mexican president Claudia Sheinbaum agreed to station ten thousand Mexican soldiers on the US-Mexico border. Trump postponed the tariffs, reinstated them, and then postponed them again. Although chaotic, Trump's maneuvers appeared to achieve the desired outcome. With Mexico's help, illegal crossings at the southern border in February and March 2025 were down 94 percent from the same months in the prior year.

Tariffs and Trade Wars

When applied selectively and thoughtfully, tariffs can help to decrease or eliminate trade imbalances. When applied haphazardly, tariffs can lead to economic chaos and a damaging trade war. A trade imbalance occurs when a country's imports and exports are not equal, resulting in either a trade surplus (when exports exceed imports) or a trade deficit (when imports exceed exports). In 2024 the United States had the world's largest annual trade deficit, totaling more than $1.2 trillion. On April 2, 2025, Trump announced tariffs that he contended were aimed at correcting trade imbalances with all other countries. The United States would charge a tariff rate of 10 percent on all countries. Countries that levy higher tariffs on the United States would be charged higher tariffs. The new tariffs were about 50 percent smaller than the tariffs that most foreign counties placed on American goods. For example, the European Union places 39 percent tariffs on American imports. Under the new tariffs, the United States would charge the European Union 20 percent.

Trump's Second Inaugural Address

On January 20, 2025, Donald Trump gave his second inaugural address. In it, he called for a revival of America's pioneering spirit:

> The United States will once again consider itself a growing nation, one that increases our wealth, expands our territory, builds our cities, raises our expectations, and carries our flag into new and beautiful horizons. . . .
>
> There's no nation like our nation. Americans are explorers, builders, innovators, entrepreneurs, and pioneers. The spirit of the frontier is written into our hearts. The call of the next great adventure resounds from within our souls. Our American ancestors turned a small group of colonies on the edge of a vast continent into a mighty republic of the most extraordinary citizens on Earth. No one comes close.
>
> Americans pushed thousands of miles through a rugged land of untamed wilderness. They crossed deserts, scaled mountains, braved untold dangers, won the Wild West, ended slavery, rescued millions from tyranny, lifted millions from poverty, harnessed electricity, split the atom, launched mankind into the heavens, and put the universe of human knowledge into the palm of the human hand. If we work together, there is nothing we cannot do and no dream we cannot achieve.

Donald J. Trump, "The Inaugural Address," White House, January 20, 2025. www.whitehouse.gov.

Trump's tariff announcement rocked global markets. Worried that tariffs would adversely affect multinational corporations, many investors sold stocks they held in vulnerable businesses. After several days of market uncertainty, Trump announced a ninety-day pause on the tariffs above 10 percent for all countries except for China, Mexico, and Canada. Critics attacked Trump for igniting a trade war and increasing the cost of imported goods. "[English political and social critic] G.K. Chesterton said that civilizations decline when they forget the obvious things, and one of the obvious things is that tariffs are really bad for a country," observed conservative columnist David Brooks. "All the things you want in an economy that are good, get worse under tariffs. You get lower wages. You get lower productivity. You get lower supply chain flows. So, to me, it's a self-destructive policy."[41]

Dismantling Federal Agencies

Another factor hurting American competitiveness, Trump believes, is the federal debt. Every year since 2001, the federal government has spent more than it has taken in. To meet its obligations, the government has to borrow money. By 2025 the total national debt stood at $36.22 trillion. The new tariffs were designed to help balance the budget and even pay down the national debt.

Another way of reducing deficits is to cut government spending. During the presidential campaign, Trump spoke often about reining in government spending. Since taking office, he has embarked on a campaign to make good on his promise. His strategy involves eliminating entire federal agencies, ending US aid to other nations, and firing hundreds of thousands of federal workers. To carry out this strategy, Trump enlisted the help of the world's wealthiest person, Elon Musk. Musk is the chief executive officer of carmaker Tesla and the rocket manufacturer SpaceX. Trump put Musk in charge of the Department of Government Efficiency (DOGE), a newly created agency within the federal government. Musk (who was not being

With Trump's blessing, billionaire Elon Musk (pictured in 2025 in the White House Oval Office) has eliminated dozens of essential federal agencies and fired hundreds of thousands of workers in health, science, education, foreign aid, veterans affairs, and more.

paid for his work) and his staff of mostly young software engineers spent months combing through government records to, as Musk tells it, identify and dismantle wasteful programs.

In the first two months of the Trump presidency, Musk's group fired about twenty-five thousand probationary employees from multiple US government agencies and departments. The Trump administration further ordered those agencies and departments to eliminate hundreds of thousands more jobs from their remaining workforces. According to the online business news website Government Executive, the affected agencies include the US Department of Defense, the US Department of Veterans Affairs, the US Environmental Protection Agency, the US Department of Education, the National Institutes of Health, the National Aeronautics and Space Administration, and the US Agency for International Development. The goal, Musk said, was to cut $1 trillion to $2 trillion in government spending.

Many legal scholars questioned the constitutionality of a president using his executive powers to dismantle agencies created by Congress. Other scholars questioned the legality of accessing sensitive data to identify jobs and contracts for the chopping block. Dozens of lawsuits have been filed against the Trump administration. Federal judges have blocked some of the actions taken by DOGE. Those cases have been appealed. Federal appellate courts have ruled in favor of the Trump administration in some cases, such as shutting down the US Agency for International Development, which is the principal US government agency responsible for administering foreign aid and development assistance. Federal appellate courts have ruled against it in others, including DOGE's attempt to access sensitive Social Security data. Many if not all of these lawsuits will likely make their way to the Supreme Court for a final resolution.

Rhetoric or Recklessness?

Trump also set off alarm bells when he said that the United States should acquire Greenland and take back control of the Panama

Canal for national defense purposes. When pressed by reporters, he refused to rule out the use of military force to accomplish these ends. Some analysts believe Trump's reckless words have the potential to draw the United States into armed conflicts. Others believe he is using the same tactics he did to persuade Mexico and Canada to boost security at the borders. Historian Victor Davis Hanson argues that Trump's tactics are a lot more sophisticated than they seem:

> He's very clever. He does certain things that [his critics] don't understand. All of this stuff about . . . Greenland and Panama . . . they all wrote it off as just nutty. . . . It's not so much the objective. It's the dialogue that follows. He says "Greenland," and everybody says he's an imperialist. And then they start thinking about it and they say: "You know, in World War II, the United States under Roosevelt pretty much appropriated the Greenland coastline for anti-submarine and air use." And then people start writing: "Well, wait a minute, New York is closer to Greenland than is Copenhagen. Well, wait a minute, Greenland, is part of North America it's not part of Europe." . . . That's what he intends—not invading Greenland or sending the 101st [Airborne Division] down to Panama. But it starts to move the needle on all of these issues.[42]

Whatever he says and whatever he does, Trump will remain a lightning rod for controversy. His critics will accuse him of lying, while his supporters will listen to the same words and say he exaggerates for effect. His critics will say he is inciting hatred, while his supporters will argue he is dealing in harsh truths. His opponents will say he only cares about himself, but his supporters believe he cares about them and speaks for them. Only

"All of this stuff about . . . Greenland and Panama . . . they all wrote it off as just nutty. . . . It's not so much the objective. It's the dialogue that follows."[42]

—Victor Davis Hanson, historian

Seeking Peace in Ukraine

On February 24, 2022, the military forces of Russia invaded Ukraine. Three years later, the war was still raging. From his first days in office, Trump has said he wants the Russia-Ukraine war to end. In his address to a joint session of Congress, he said, "It's time to stop this madness. It's time to halt the killing. It's time to end this senseless war. If you want to end wars, you have to talk to both sides."

Trump hoped to negotiate an immediate end to all hostilities. That did not work, so he changed course. In March 2025 he began pursuing limited cease-fires that might eventually lead to a full peace. Ukraine and Russia okayed a proposal to end attacks on each other's energy infrastructure, but that deal fell through. Next, both sides agreed to allow commercial shipping to resume in the Black Sea, but the success of this agreement remained uncertain. Russia has a long list of conditions that must be met before any agreement takes effect. Many European leaders were skeptical that Trump's efforts would bear fruit, but Trump remained optimistic that a deal could be reached to end the loss of lives on both sides.

Donald J. Trump, "Remarks by President Trump in Joint Address to Congress," White House, March 6, 2025. www.whitehouse.gov.

one thing remains certain: Donald Trump says he has a mandate to bring change to the federal government and to American society as a whole. He already has changed the makeup of his party and redrawn the electoral map. In the early days of his second term, he has taken steps to change government at home and relations abroad. There are certainly more changes to come.

1946

Donald John Trump is born on June 14 in New York City.

1970

Trump begins working with his father developing real estate in Queens and Brooklyn.

1977

Donald Trump marries Ivana Zelníčková.

1980

Trump's first New York City development, the Grand Hyatt Hotel, opens.

1983

Trump Tower opens on Fifth Avenue in Manhattan.

1987

Trump's bestselling book, *Trump: The Art of the Deal*, is published.

1993

After divorcing his first wife, Trump marries Marla Maples.

1996

Trump purchases the Miss Universe, Miss USA, and Miss Teen USA pageants.

2004

The reality show *The Apprentice*, with Trump as host, debuts on NBC.

2005

After divorcing his second wife, Trump marries Melania Knauss.

2015

Trump announces his intention to run for president in a June speech at Trump Tower in New York.

2016

Trump wins the presidential election.

2017

Trump is sworn in as the forty-fifth president of the United States.

2019

In December, the US House of Representatives impeaches Trump for abuse of power and obstruction of Congress over allegations that he improperly sought help from Ukraine to boost his chances of reelection; he is acquitted by the Senate in 2020.

2020

Trump loses his presidential reelection bid.

2021

In January, Trump is impeached a second time. This time he is charged with incitement of insurrection in connection with the January 6 attack on the US Capitol; he is acquitted by the Senate in February.

2023

Trump is indicted on thirty-four criminal charges of falsifying business records in a scheme to illegally influence the 2016 election.

2024

Following a trial in New York, in May a jury finds Trump guilty of all thirty-four felony charges; in November Trump is elected to a second term as president.

2025

Trump is sworn in as the forty-seventh president of the United States.

Introduction: A Striking Turnaround

1. Quoted in Brian Naylor, "Read Trump's Jan. 6 Speech, a Key Part of Impeachment Trial," NPR, February 10, 2021. www.npr.org.
2. Donald J. Trump, "The Inaugural Address," White House, January 20, 2025. www.whitehouse.gov.
3. Donald J. Trump, "Initial Rescissions of Harmful Executive Orders and Actions," White House, January 20, 2025. www.whitehouse.gov.
4. Quoted in *PBS NewsHour*, *WATCH: Trump Signs More Executive Orders on His First Night Back in the Oval Office*, YouTube, January 20, 2025. www.youtube.com/watch?v=GX-gtXdnPwU&t=14s.
5. Editorial board, "Trump's Opening Act of Contempt," *New York Times*, January 20, 2025. www.nytimes.com.

Chapter One: From Childhood Rebel to Young Millionaire

6. Donald Trump and Tony Schwartz, *Trump: The Art of the Deal*. New York: Ballantine, 1987, p. 65.
7. Quoted in Jason Horowitz, "Fred Trump Taught His Son the Essentials of Showboating Self-Promotion," *New York Times*, August 12, 2016. www.nytimes.com.
8. Quoted in Horowitz, "Fred Trump Taught His Son the Essentials of Showboating Self-Promotion."
9. Trump and Schwartz, *Trump*, p. 74.
10. Trump and Schwartz, *Trump*, p. 79.
11. Quoted in Trump and Schwartz, *Trump*, p. 79.
12. Quoted in Trump and Schwartz, *Trump*, p. 79.
13. Quoted in Marc Fisher, "Growing Up Trump," *Moment Magazine*, May 24, 2017. https://medium.com.
14. Quoted in Trump and Schwartz, *Trump*, p. 72.
15. Quoted in Trump and Schwartz, *Trump*, p. 76.

Chapter Two: Trump's Early Career

16. Quoted in Trump and Schwartz, *Trump*, p. 105.
17. Trump and Schwartz, *Trump*, p. 73.
18. Prachi Gupta, "6 Things You Need to Know About Donald Trump's First Wife, Ivana," *Cosmopolitan*, April 8, 2016. www.cosmopolitan.com.
19. Quoted in Ilan Ben-Meir, "That Time Trump Spent Nearly $100,000 on an Ad Criticizing U.S. Foreign Policy in 1987," BuzzFeed, July 11, 2015. www.buzzfeednews.com.
20. Quoted in Ben-Meir, "That Time Trump Spent Nearly $100,000 on an Ad Criticizing U.S. Foreign Policy in 1987."
21. Quoted in OWN, "Donald Trump Teases a President Bid During a 1988 Oprah Show," YouTube, June 26, 2015. www.youtube.com/watch?v=SEPs17_AkTI.
22. Quoted in OWN, "Donald Trump Teases a President Bid During a 1988 Oprah Show."
23. Quoted in Robert Shogan, "Buchanan Starts 'America First' Bid for President," *Los Angeles Times*, December 11, 1991. www.latimes.com.

Chapter Three: Trump's First Term

24. Quoted in *Time* staff, "Here's Donald Trump's Presidential Announcement Speech," *Time*, June 16, 2015. https://time.com.
25. Rush Limbaugh, "Trump's Message Will Resonate," The Rush Limbaugh Show, June 16, 2015. www.rushlimbaugh.com.
26. Quoted in Kim Gittleson, "US Tax Cuts: Are They the Biggest in American History?," BBC, April 17, 2018. www.bbc.com.
27. Quoted in Alana Wise et al., "Where It Stands: Election Hinges on Key States, Final Results May Take a While," NPR, November 3, 2020. www.npr.org.
28. Quoted in Wise et al., "Where It Stands."
29. Quoted in Naylor, "Read Trump's Jan. 6 Speech, a Key Part of Impeachment Trial."
30. Quoted in Barbara Sprunt, "7 GOP Senators Voted to Convict Trump. Only 1 Faces Voters Next Year," NPR, February 15, 2021. www.npr.org.

Chapter Four: A Second Run for the White House

31. Quoted in Geoff Bennett, "Bill Barr: Trump Committed a 'Grave Wrongdoing' in Jan. 6 Case," *PBS NewsHour*, August 4, 2023. www.pbs.org.
32. Quoted in Anthony Zurcher, "How Donald Trump Came Back from the Political Abyss," BBC, November 2, 2024. www.bbc.com.
33. Quoted in Ali Vitali and Allan Smith, "Trump CPAC Speech Revives 'Rigged' Election Lie, Declares Political Journey 'Far from Over,'" NBC News, March 1, 2021. www.nbcnews.com.
34. Quoted in CNN staff, "READ: Biden-Trump Debate Transcript," CNN, June 28, 2024. https://edition.cnn.com.
35. Quoted in CNN staff, "READ."
36. Quoted in Daniel Marans, "The TV Moment That Might Have Been Kamala Harris' Biggest Mistake," HuffPost, November 11, 2024. www.huffpost.com.
37. Quoted in Marans, "The TV Moment That Might Have Been Kamala Harris' Biggest Mistake."

Chapter Five: Winning the Presidency a Second Time

38. Quoted in Dan Mangan, "Trump Declares Victory Hours Before Clearing Electoral College Threshold Against Harris," CNBC, November 6, 2024. www.cnbc.com.
39. Quoted in Stephanie Murray et al., "Trump's Cabinet Picks Are Generating Controversy. For His Supporters, They're Just Right," *USA Today*, December 17, 2024. www.usatoday.com.
40. Quoted in Ellie Quinlan Houghtaling, "Trump's Real Goal With These Disastrous Cabinet Picks," *New Republic*, November 18, 2024. https://newrepublic.com.
41. Quoted in *PBS NewsHour*, *Brooks and Capehart on Trump's New Tariffs and Spending Freeze Chaos*, YouTube, February 1, 2025. https://youtu.be/jMi6_cC0xc8?si=1pjoYCEuBYwcZ_Hv.
42. Quoted in GBNews, *Victor Davis Hanson on Trump's Unstoppable Rise to Power*, YouTube, January 22, 2025. https://youtu.be/GstoRlioBuQ?si=eTSkKBAvxpdau3jE.

Books

Stephen Currie, *Joe Biden: 46th US President*. San Diego, CA: ReferencePoint, 2021.

Victor Davis Hanson, *The Case for Trump*. New York: Basic Books, 2024.

Naomi Rockler, *American Democracy in Crisis*. San Diego, CA: ReferencePoint, 2024.

James Roland, *Kamala Harris: History-Making US Vice President*. San Diego, CA: ReferencePoint, 2021.

Ramin Setoodeh, *Apprentice in Wonderland: How Donald Trump and Mark Burnett Took America Through the Looking Glass*. New York: Harper, 2024.

Jill C. Wheeler, *Donald Trump*. Minneapolis, MN: Checkerboard Library, 2024.

Bob Woodward and Robert Costa, *Peril*. New York: Simon & Schuster, 2021.

Internet Sources

CNN staff, "READ: Biden-Trump Debate Transcript," CNN, June 28, 2024. https://edition.cnn.com.

Riley Hoffman, "READ: Harris-Trump Presidential Debate Transcript," ABC News, September 11, 2024. https://abcnews.go.com.

National Archives and Records Administration, "What Is the Electoral College?," November 4, 2024. www.archives.gov.

Brian Naylor, "Read Trump's Jan. 6 Speech, a Key Part of Impeachment Trial," NPR, February 10, 2021. www.npr.org.

Time staff, "Here's Donald Trump's Presidential Announcement Speech," *Time*, June 16, 2015. http://time.com.

Donald J. Trump, "The Inaugural Address," White House, January 20, 2025. www.whitehouse.gov.

Anthony Zurcher, "How Donald Trump Came Back from the Political Abyss," BBC, November 2, 2024. www.bbc.com.

Websites

Donald Trump, ABC News
http://abcnews.go.com/topics/news/donald-trump.htm
The latest news and in-depth coverage of Trump by ABC News, with headlines, photos, and videos.

Donald Trump, PolitiFact
www.politifact.com/personalities/donald-trump
The nonpartisan website PolitiFact fact-checks Trump's statements and keeps a running tally on how many are true, mostly true, false, and "Pants on Fire," or totally false.

Election 2024: Presidential Results, CNN
www.cnn.com/election/2024/results/president
This CNN web page provides information about the states won by each candidate, along with popular vote totals and information about congressional races.

White House
www.whitehouse.gov
The federal government's official presidential website, with speeches, press releases, policy positions, and other information.

Note: Boldface page numbers indicate illustrations.

PICTURE CREDITS

Cover: Associated Press

5: CNP/AdMedia/Newscom
10: Photo by John Barrett/PHOTOlink/Newscom
13: Seth Poppel/ZUMA Press/Newscom
15: Anne Kitzman/Shutterstock
18: World History Archive/Alamy Stock Photo
21: Wangkun Jia/Shutterstock
23: Chris Willson/Alamy Stock Photo
28: Dennis Van Tine/STAR MAX/IPx
32: Benjamin Clapp/Shutterstock
34: Associated Press
37: Brian Cahn/ZUMAPRESS/Newscom
41: David Peinado Romero/Shutterstock
44: Maxim Elramsisy/Alamy Stock Photo
47: Joe Marino/UPI/Newscom
48: Associated Press
52: Associated Press

ABOUT THE AUTHOR

Bradley Steffens is a novelist, a poet, and an award-winning author of more than seventy nonfiction books for children and young adults.